Original title:
A Thousand Tiny Twigs

Author: Eleanor Prescott
ISBN HARDBACK: 978-1-80567-281-4
ISBN PAPERBACK: 978-1-80567-580-8

The Artistry of Altered Landscapes

In the garden, sticks abound,
They dance around without a sound.
With clever hands, I start my play,
Transform these twigs in a witty way.

Bending low, then swooping high,
Each branch a tale, under the sky.
A fence, a chair, or maybe a hat,
Watch them giggle, how about that?

Whispering Roots and Wayward Vines

Roots with secrets, buried low,
Vines that wander, putting on a show.
They tangle up, they twist and shout,
In this laughter, there's no doubt.

“Where’s my shoe?” a vine will tease,
“Right here!” it’ll say, with playful ease.
Each curl and crook has stories distill,
Of all the antics, oh what a thrill!

Mosaic of Miniature Memories

Collecting bits from here and there,
Sticks and stones, with so much flair.
Each piece has history, a tale to weave,
In this craft, the heart believes.

Snipping here and gluing there,
I swear my fingers are beyond repair!
Creating magic from what's mundane,
A strange, fun mess, but what's to gain?

Realm of Resilient Remnants

From remnants left after the storm,
New adventures begin to form.
A crooked staff, a funny hat,
All from sticks, where the laughter’s at.

In the realm where the broken play,
Every piece holds a silly sway.
In the chaos, I sense a charm,
With every twig, there's joy to warm.

Echoes Beneath the Canopy

In the woods where whispers play,
Squirrels chat and dance all day.
Leaves giggle under tiny feet,
As nature hums a playful beat.

A raccoon snickers at a flop,
While rabbits bounce in a happy hop.
Birds throw jokes from high above,
Mistakes are made, but all is love.

Beneath the Bark and Leaf

Under bark, a funny crew,
Mice in capes, making their debut.
When a worm slides by in style,
The toads all pause, then grin a smile.

A snail slips on a leafy stage,
Declaring boldly, "I'm the sage!"
But in the race, oh what a sight,
He loses to a beetle's flight.

The Tapestry of Twigs

Twigs and sticks form stories grand,
Of dance-offs held in the woodland band.
A fox shows moves, all slick and sly,
While a porcupine gives it a try.

The laughter echoes, fills the air,
As everyone joins in without a care.
But who will win, the crowd can’t tell,
In this twiggy tale, we laugh so well.

Secrets in the Underbrush

In the underbrush, secrets unfold,
With ladybugs recounting tales of old.
A hedgehog whispers, “You won't believe,
I once caught a leaf, thought it was a thief!”

Beneath the ferns, a party brews,
With tiny drinks made of morning dew.
A party hat made of a cap,
And everyone laughs at a napping chap.

Fractals of Nature's Kiss

In the garden of giggles,
Little sticks hold a chat,
They gossip like the wind,
About the latest hat.

Frogs wear crowns made of leaves,
And dance on the muddy trails,
While bees buzz sweet melodies,
Spreading joy with their tales.

Health of the Fragments

Branches stretch to the sky,
Each twig claims a small dream,
Chasing after the butterflies,
In a world made of cream.

A squirrel dons tiny glasses,
Reading recipes from trees,
Cooking acorns for his friends,
While they giggle with ease.

Unearthed Whispers

Rustling leaves share secrets,
Of the silly ants on the run,
Wearing tiny sombreros,
Joking ‘bout the sun.

Each twig a storyteller,
Telling tales of the day,
Of mud pies and splashes,
In a fun, frothy play.

Nature's Fleeting Thoughts

Floaty clouds play hopscotch,
With sunbeams on the ground,
As twigs get tangled in laughter,
With every bouncy bound.

The moon peeks through branches,
Winking like an old friend,
Sharing late-night secrets,
As the day starts to end.

The Secrets in the Shadows

In the woods where whispers play,
The shadows dance, then hide away.
A squirrel with a secret grin,
Mischief waits for night to win.

Branches with stories, tales untold,
Twisted paths, adventures bold.
A raccoon wears a mask so sly,
While crickets laugh as shadows fly.

Sifting Through Sylvan Shards

Fallen leaves like gold confetti,
Pine cones roll, oh so unsteady.
Hopping here and there with glee,
A chipmunk mocks the tall old tree.

Glimmers sparkle in the light,
Nature's sparkle in full sight.
Twigs fall down, an acorn slips,
Watch your step, or you'll get nips!

Whispers of Woodland Steps

Follow squirrels with bouncing tails,
Through the shade where laughter sails.
Unexpected laughs from every nook,
Mischievous eyes in every crook.

Hopping frogs in suits of green,
Waddle past, what a sight to glean.
Old logs whisper silly tales,
As friendly foxes prance in trails.

Fragments of Nature's Embrace

In a world of tangled charm,
A butterfly, with grace, disarms.
Frogs jump high, while owls just stare,
What secrets float in woodland air?

Chickadees chirp a funny tune,
While shadows giggle under moon.
Twigs and leaves in a goofy dance,
Nature's stage, a wild romance.

Stalwart Spirits Beneath the Canopy

Beneath the leafy shield, they squeal,
Squirrels in a race, what's the deal?
Twigs wagging in the playful breeze,
Nature’s jesters dance with ease.

Bark-clad gnomes play peek-a-boo,
With every rustle, a laugh anew.
Roots tickle toes when you take a stroll,
Join the woodland prank, that's the goal!

Twigs in the Twilight

In twilight's glow, they start to jive,
Twigs wiggling as if alive.
Crickets chirp the woodland tune,
As shadows sway beneath the moon.

Branches gossip, sharing grins,
As chipmunks plot their silly wins.
A twig-tastic party, everyone’s in,
Laughing and twirling, let the fun begin!

Fingers of the Earth

The earth has fingers, oh so sly,
Tickling roots as they wave goodbye.
Worms roll by in a slimy spree,
Wiggling their way, oh what a spree!

Grass blades giggle in gentle play,
Hiding secrets from light of day.
Each little bump, a hidden jest,
In this green realm, they're hardly rest!

Weathered Wisdom of Woodland

Old trees whisper of days gone past,
With bark so wise, their tales will last.
A branch might chuckle, a leaf might nod,
Nature's humor, a lilting prod.

Mushrooms tease from their mossy beds,
“Why not dance?” the old oak spreads.
A raucous laugh echoes through the leaves,
In this wild place, everyone believes!

Nature's Humble Poetry

In the forest, sticks do lie,
With secrets whispered by and by.
Each small twig holds a joke untold,
Of squirrels who dance and rabbits bold.

A branch once waved a grand hello,
But tripped on roots and fell below.
The acorns giggle, rolling away,
As leaves gossip, come out to play.

Every Stick Tells a Tale

A stick shaped like a crooked nose,
Claims to know where the best cheese grows.
The bark is rough with stories vast,
Of birds that chirp and shadows cast.

One slender limb thinks it can sing,
But all it does is jabber and fling.
Woodpeckers nod, saying, 'Give it a rest!'
While ants debate who’s truly the best.

Beyond the Timber's Edge

In a glen where the wild things frolic,
Twigs chat about the day's iconic.
A stick made jokes, oh what a sight,
As squirrels threw acorns in delight.

A twig once stood with a crown so grand,
Claiming it ruled this wooded land.
But tripped on its royal bark so thick,
And fell right down, oh what a trick!

Tiny Tendrils of Hope

A sprout crawled out with dreams so high,
Said, 'Watch me reach for the bright blue sky!'
The winds laughed hard, swirling all around,
Saying, 'Don’t rush, just stay on the ground!'

With each little twist, it learned to bend,
Fashioned a crown, it called a friend.
In the humor of growth, life starts to trip,
But hope remains, a sturdy little grip.

Nature's Fibers in Flight

In the breeze, they take a ride,
Dancing on the mountainside.
Each little stick a tiny wand,
Casting spells that go beyond.

With a flick, they twist and twirl,
Turning leaves into a whirl.
Nature's own silly parade,
Unruly forms that never fade.

They jive and jump, they poke and prod,
An orchestra of nature's nod.
Up in the air, they spin around,
Tickling noses, they astound!

From branches high, they take their cue,
A playful dance with a lively crew.
Laughter rustles where they're strewn,
All around, the twigs commune!

The Murmur of Minimalism

In the stillness, whispers creep,
Twirling twigs that never sleep.
Each a secret, quietly told,
Adventures in woodlands bold.

A lone twig struts like a star,
Claiming the ground, oh so bizarre!
Underfoot, the critters scamper,
Tiny twigs make minimal hamper.

Caterpillars play hide and seek,
Among the fibers, so unique.
Nature giggles at their game,
Miniature sticks, no one's to blame.

The oddest shapes, a laughing bunch,
With twirling moves that make us brunch!
They chatter softly, day and night,
Murmurs of joy, a funny sight.

Interwoven Tales of the Terrain

In the forest, tales are spun,
Every twig a story begun.
A web of giggles, knots and bends,
Nature's laughter never ends.

A twig meets leaf, they gossip away,
Sharing secrets in disarray.
"Look at you!" says one with flair,
"Fancy a dance? Do you dare?"

Each curve and line, a plot unfolds,
Twigs in funny hats, truth be told.
A jester's cap, a royal crown,
Who knew they'd be the talk of town?

They spin and sway, a comic show,
Nature's quirks all on display.
As sunbeams tickle every scene,
Twigs unite, a joyful glean!

Silhouettes in the Underbrush

In the dusk, they cast their shade,
Bobbing gently, they invade.
Silly shapes against the night,
Twigs in costumes, pure delight.

A shadow dance, they twist and sway,
Joking with the stars at play.
Each little branch, a silent jest,
Nature’s humor, in its best.

From the ground, they catch a breeze,
Nudging insects with such ease.
“Hey you there!” one twig shouts loud,
“Join our party, we’re all proud!”

In the underbrush, they roam free,
Jigging joyfully, full of glee.
Twigs of laughter, night’s embrace,
A hidden ball where critters race!

Kaleidoscope of Twigs

Twigs of many hues align,
A lively dance, a fun design.
They twirl and spin, a sight so bright,
Tiny sticks bring pure delight.

Bending left, then bending right,
Twiggy critters take their flight.
Each little piece a tale conceals,
Of mischief done and squeaky squeals.

With a flick, a twist, a turn,
Crafting shapes for all to learn.
A bundle here, a bunch not there,
What a jolly twiggish affair!

Let’s gather 'round, let giggles soar,
For each small stick holds tales galore.
In nature’s hand, the laughter clings,
A chorus sung by twiggy things.

The Elegance of Subtle Sticks

In the garden where they lay,
Subtle sticks have much to say.
With graceful bows and cheeky prance,
They host a twiggy, silly dance.

With each little nudge and playful poke,
These sticks propose, a splendid joke.
Who knew such elegance could be,
Just a branch, a leaf, a glee?

They whisper softly to the breeze,
Chasing ants with charming ease.
How formal dance when stuff's askew,
Nature's mischief in every view.

So next time you see twigs around,
Remember, they’re for laughter found.
In every crack, a giggle’s near,
Just bend down and lend an ear.

Nature's Minuscule Masterpieces

Amidst the grass, they poke and prod,
Little sticks look quite shoddy, odd.
Yet in their humble, quirky way,
They cheer us up with much to say.

Each tiny twig a crafty muse,
In a jigsaw puzzle, they amuse.
With crooked lines and patches worn,
They tell the tales of laughter born.

In twirling forms, they mimic fate,
A gaggle of fun in every state.
Watch as they gather, form a crowd,
Yelling "Look at us!" oh so loud!

With every rustle, every shake,
These minuscule bits surely partake.
In nature's laughter, oh so bright,
They inch away into the night.

Whittle Away the Silence

Let’s whittle, twist, and turn away,
The silence here is far too gray.
With tiny twigs and clever flair,
We craft a ruckus, fill the air.

In every cut, a laugh is born,
A critter jumps, a leaf is torn.
Each carve reveals a new surprise,
In silent woods, we improvise.

A tickle here, a poke right there,
A little twig becomes a chair.
For fairies, sprites, and ants to dwell,
In our giggles, all is swell.

So whittle down that silence now,
With every stick, take a bow.
In woods of joy, we surely thrive,
Through tiny twigs, we come alive.

The Sweetness of Small

In a world so vast and wide,
Little things dance with pride.
A crumb on the floor, a speck of dust,
In their tiny kingdom, we must trust.

A thimble hat for the playful ant,
They march in line, the merry chant.
With acorns as cars, they zoom about,
In the tiniest realm, there’s no doubt.

A drizzle of rain’s their grand parade,
Splashing through puddles, unafraid.
Each drop, a party, they twirl and spin,
In a life so small, there’s joy within.

So here’s to the wee, the fun, the spry,
With a little wink, they’ll reach for the sky.
For in the simple, silly, and small,
Lies the sweetest laughter of all.

Paths Woven in Shadows

In the forest where shadows dance,
Little footsteps take a chance.
Branches bend, a sway and a twist,
Creating a trail not easily missed.

The squirrels giggle, racing along,
With acorn hats, they sing their song.
A rabbit hops, with a sudden lark,
Leaving shadows where it left its mark.

Down a hollow, a secret lane,
Home to whispers of playful rain.
In each nook, a jest awaits,
Life's a jest, oh, how it sedates!

So follow the giggles, the chuckles and cheers,
Where shadows weave and slice through fears.
In this quirky dance of nature's grace,
A funny tale spins in an endless chase.

The Flight of the Fragile

Once a twig thought it could fly,
With wings of dreams, it soared the sky.
But with a gust, it tumbled down,
Into a puddle, what a frown!

Dandelion fluff, a fragile kite,
Took to the wind in sheer delight.
But just when it thought it had a chance,
A gust played a trick, it's lost in the dance.

Ladybugs in tiny suits rejoice,
With little giggles, they make their choice.
A leap to the air, a flippery flop,
In the world of small, it’s a perfect drop.

So raise a toast to the frail and small,
For in their blunders, we see it all.
With every tumble, every trip,
Life’s a giggle with each little blip.

Gentle Reminders in the Woods

In the woods where giggles thrive,
A troupe of critters come alive.
Whispers float from leaf to leaf,
A comic tale, a playful brief.

The sly old fox in mismatched shoes,
Trips over roots, a humorous muse.
In search of dinner, he takes a spin,
Yet finds himself ensnared in a whim!

Bunny hops with a cheeky grin,
“Chasing shadows? Where to begin?”
With every tumble, a lesson taught,
In the forest’s embrace, joy is sought.

Each twig’s a laugh, each leaf’s a cheer,
Echoes of fun ring distant and near.
In this woodland world, take heart, be bold,
Embrace the giggles that nature unfolds.

Whispers of Weathered Wood

In the breeze, they chatter loud,
Old branches say, "Look, I’m a cloud!"
Leaves gossip, rustle without care,
Woodpeckers drum a beat so rare.

Rabbits hop on roots, oh so spry,
Squirrels plan mischief from up high.
A tree stump grumbles, "I’m quite a seat!"
Nature’s bench, where all critters meet.

Moss laughs as it blankets all around,
With snickers that can't help but abound.
Twigs play tic-tac-toe on the ground,
In a world where joy can always be found.

So skip through the forest, embrace the odd,
Join in the dance and give a nod!
For every branch that bends and sways,
Holds a secret of quirky play days.

Fragments of Nature's Kaleidoscope

Watch the leaves tumble and spin,
Playing hide and seek, they grin.
A frog leaps, in a hopscotch game,
While the sun's rays put him to shame.

Acorns roll like little balls,
Nature's marbles, no need for walls.
Butterflies flutter by with flair,
As crickets join in with their fair share.

The wind tells tales of lovesick vines,
Who twirl and twist, drawn by the signs.
With every rustle, a chuckle is caught,
In this patchwork of glee, life's a riotous plot!

So gather your laughter, splash in the green,
With petals and petals, oh what a scene!
This riot of colors, a joyful spree,
Fragments of life that set nature free.

The Dance of Delicate Branches

Branches sway like they dance ballet,
With squirrels stealing the show all day!
A feathered choir croons from up high,
While ants march in line, oh my oh my!

The breeze tickles leaves, causing a giggle,
As shadows play tag beneath the wiggle.
Each twig jumps in, surprising a foe,
Tickling toes as they stomp in a row.

A raccoon prances, cheeky and bold,
Stealing sweet berries offering gold.
A wild rumpus with friends all around,
In this theater where fun is profound.

So let's join the branchets and sway to their tune,
Under the watchful eye of the moon.
It's a party of twigs who laugh with glee,
Embracing the madness of nature's spree.

Echoes of Ancient Bark

Stumps tell tales of days gone by,
Of whispers shared beneath the sky.
A woodpecker ponders, "What’s the fuss?"
As branches echo in a curious rush.

The bark is wise, it chuckles and sighs,
With wrinkles that hold the sun and skies.
Mice tell stories, huddled so tight,
Of moonlit feasts and shadows at night.

Fungi giggle, sprouting in flocks,
Joining the joke in woodland socks.
With every ring, life circles anew,
A hilarity spun from nature’s own view.

So come, dear friend, lend your ear,
To the echoes of laughter we hold so dear.
For in every knot and dent we create,
Lies a symphony of joy to celebrate.

Delicate Connections

In the woods where critters play,
Little branches dance and sway.
A squirrel's hop, a bird's quick dive,
It’s a jungle gym where all survive.

Lizards scamper near the ground,
Balancing tricks, they’re quite profound.
Grasshoppers leap in silly bounds,
Nature’s laughter knows no sounds.

Winding twigs in knotty curls,
Create a maze where fun unfurls.
With each twist, a tale does grow,
Of little joys that steal the show.

Underneath the shaded trees,
Life's a game with gentle breeze.
Every leaf, a giggle shared,
In their world, nothing's bared.

Nature's Intricate Web

In tangled lines where critters soar,
Each tiny twig is never a bore.
Spiders weaving grand designs,
A sticky joke that brightly shines.

Ants on missions, hats in hand,
Marching through this twiggy land.
Their tiny feet in rhythm pound,
A parade where joy abounds.

Beetles rolling tiny balls,
Playing games amid the stalls.
With laughter high and spirits free,
They spin their tales beneath the tree.

Under skies of blue and gray,
Nature giggles, come what may.
Threads of fun in every twist,
In this web, you can’t resist.

The Symphony of Small Branches

Beneath the canopy they play,
Little sticks just want to sway.
With nature’s tunes and breezy rhymes,
They jazz it up with funny times.

Chipmunks strum on hollow barks,
Dancing madly, leaving marks.
Branches sway in funny beats,
Nature's rhythm, oh, so sweet.

A hopping frog joins in the fun,
Splashing notes under the sun.
Each pluck of twig, a comic flare,
In their world, without a care.

Twisted limbs, their stories blend,
Each silly jig, a happy trend.
Singing hearts in leafy shade,
Here all giggles are displayed.

Grounded Dreams of the Forest

From mossy beds where dreams are spun,
Little twigs form paths for fun.
A rabbit hops, a fox prances,
Life’s a stage with funny chances.

Beneath the ferns, a secret scheme,
Where every branch can dare to dream.
Wise old owls with feathers bright,
Chuckle softly through the night.

With gentle nudges from the earth,
Each tiny twig boasts of worth.
Creating worlds, they simply do,
With little thoughts and laughter too.

So join the dance and twirl about,
In nature's home, there's no doubt.
With each connection, it’s revealed,
Life's the punchline, always sealed.

Rustic Remnants

In the garden, sticks abound,
They trip my feet upon the ground.
A crooked stick, what fun it brings,
I dance and twirl like a bird with wings.

I scoop up twigs, a makeshift wand,
Pretend I'm casting spells of fond.
The neighbor's cat gives me a stare,
As if to say, 'You really dare?'

They swirl and spin in wild delight,
These humble relics of the night.
I'll build a castle, tall and grand,
With nothing but this twinkling band.

Oh, what joy in simple things,
A throne for squirrels, for birds I bring.
From remnants rustic, dreams do sprout,
In every twig, I'll dance about.

Starlit Twigs and Moonlit Nights

Beneath the stars, I find my path,
With twigs that tickle, my hearty laugh.
I trip on roots and giggle loud,
Imagine I'm a twiggy cloud.

The moon beams down, a silver tease,
As I twirl sticks in the evening breeze.
I try to juggle, but oh, what fun,
They scatter 'round like little suns.

With every snap, a story told,
Of woodland creatures, brave and bold.
A squirrel protests, he shakes a paw,
As I create my twiggy law.

At night, the forest starts to sway,
With twiggy chants, we dance and play.
So come, my friends, let's fill the skies,
With laughter and twigs, watch dreams arise.

The Mosaic of Nature's Craft

A collage made of tiny sticks,
Nature’s art, with many tricks.
Each piece a story, bend and sway,
In the light of a sunny day.

I build a rocket, bold and bright,
With twigs that shimmer in the light.
But suddenly, it starts to lean,
And my great conquest goes unseen.

From every heap, weird shapes emerge,
A dragon now, with fire to surge!
But oops, it falls; I laugh aloud,
A twiggy knight, oh so proud!

In nature's craft, we find our play,
With sticks and leaves, we dream away.
So gather 'round this tapestry,
Of rustic charm and mystery.

Gathered Whispers of Green

Out in the woods, I find my stash,
Of sticks and twigs—all in a flash.
They rustle softly, secrets shared,
Of woodland tales, a life declared.

I pile them high for a fairy throne,
But tripping over, I'm not alone!
With every tumble, giggles rise,
The forest echoes with surprise.

A twig in hand, I wave it round,
Declaring this my kingdom found.
The leaves applaud, the branches sway,
All hail the ruler of this play!

So join the fun, in laughter steeped,
With gathered whispers, friendships reaped.
In every twig, a story lies,
Let's bring them forth, let joy arise.

Hushed Conversations of the Wild

The squirrels chat with utmost glee,
While chipmunks laugh in harmony.
A birdie drops some nutty rhymes,
Nature's gossip, oh so sublime!

The thrush installs a secret school,
Teaching frogs how to be cool.
Leaves giggle as they sway and twirl,
In the forest, life’s a whirl!

A raccoon with a top hat struts,
Snickers at the knotted nuts.
He tells a tale of last night's feast,
And how he scared away the least!

Amidst the woods, the whispers play,
Chirps and chortles light the way.
With every nook, a chuckle spreads,
In this green land where laughter treads.

Footsteps of the Forgotten

In shadows cast by ancient trees,
Old footsteps dance upon the leaves.
Ghostly critters join the fun,
A jig for all when day is done!

The tales of yore, they tiptoe near,
As moles espouse tales we barely hear.
Once upon a midnight clear,
A rabbit squeaked, 'This dance is dear!'

Forgotten souls with furry hats,
Join the merry band of brats.
With every hop and every spin,
Past lives giggle, let the laughs begin!

A poodle forms a fancy line,
They prance and twirl, oh so divine.
In this forest soirée grand,
With twinkling stars, they take a stand!

The Life Beneath the Canopy

A beetle wears a business tie,
While ants march off to find their pie.
The worms are digging all around,
Making cozy spaces underground.

The fungi throw a mushroom bash,
Where slugs slide in with a splash.
A lively soirée, no need to pout,
In the soil, it's all about!

Creatures shuffle, chip, and grind,
Unseen laughter, one of a kind.
With tiny speakers blaring tunes,
The underground shakes, beneath the moon!

From roots to leaves, the laughter flows,
In the dark where nobody knows.
A jamboree beneath the ground,
Where every giggle knows no bound!

Entwined Echoes of Existence

In whispers soft, the branches sway,
As curious critters roam and play.
A hedgehog hums an old duet,
While rabbits hop in a froggy ballet!

Leaves laugh hard at the squirrel's prance,
And tease the fox, 'Come join the dance!'
A butterfly flits with flair and grace,
In this merry woodland place.

Hoots and caws merge as one,
As owls and crows share jokes for fun.
The shadows chuckle in the light,
In this wild hub of sheer delight.

Every sound a jumbled rhyme,
Nature’s giggles, oh so prime!
Amongst the trees, a comedy fest,
In existence's play, they jest the best!

Strands Woven in Sorrow

A stick with a twist, it spoke to a bee,
Whispers of laughter, as loud as can be.
It fell off the branch, oh where did it land?
Next to some acorns, a very weird band.

Twirling in circles, a dance on the ground,
They chuckled together, such silliness found.
But squirrels looked on, with a quizzical glance,
As twigs held a party; who knew they could prance?

The Threadbare Tapestry

A patchwork of stories, each stick has a say,
In the grand old forest, they wiggle ballet.
From the tiniest branch to the boughs in the air,
They weave and they bob, without any care.

They met with a toad, who croaked them a tune,
While ants formed a line, they danced 'neath the moon.
With laughter on leaves, they missed the sun's call,
A show with no limits, a jocular ball!

Birth of the Small

Little twigs gathered, a council was called,
To speak of their dreams, in the shadows they sprawled.
One twig with a grin, claimed it dreamed of a ship,
A vessel of fun, with the bark as the tip!

They crafted it quick, used some moss for a sail,
And soon it set off, on a grand leafy trail.
But a gust came along, oh what a surprise,
Their ship turned to splinters, they burst into cries!

Unseen Lives Among Sticks

Beneath all the chirps, and the rustle of leaves,
Are stories untold, oh, the mischief it weaves!
Twigs gathering secrets, in shadows they play,
With critters and laughter, they brighten the day.

On a pebble they perched, to discuss the great quest,
To find hidden treasures, what could be the best?
But plans often falter, as butterflies swoop,
And twigs lose their way in a cheeky loop-de-loop!

Secrets of the Undergrowth

A critter darted, what a sight,
With acorns bouncing left and right.
A squirrel slipped upon a leaf,
And swore it danced, oh what a thief!

The mushrooms giggled, pink and green,
They whispered secrets, oh so obscene.
A worm in boots slid with a grin,
Declared a party, let's begin!

Underneath the ferns so tall,
A rabbit tripped and took a fall.
With wobbly feet, it hopped around,
Like it invented silly sounds.

So join the chaos, find the fun,
Where nature's critters never shun.
In every nook, there's joy to find,
A world of giggles, truly kind!

A Carpet of Wonders

Beneath our feet, a vibrant spread,
A carpet woven, plant and thread.
Where daisies peek and clovers fold,
A treasure trove of stories told.

The ants parade in line so straight,
In oversized hats, they feel quite great.
A ladybug with dreams so big,
Takes flight and does a dizzy jig!

A beetle’s stuck, it cannot roll,
Hitching a ride, it plays the troll.
With tiny giggles, chaos looms,
In nature's realm of tiny rooms.

So step on in, explore the hue,
Find magic here, just me and you.
In all the colors of the ground,
The laughter of the wild is found!

The Heart of the Thicket

In thickets thick, the shadows dance,
Where critters play their little prance.
A fox in specs reads tales aloud,
While growing plants cheer, oh so proud!

The branches wave, a leafy cheer,
As squirrels plot their next frontier.
A brave young mouse with cheese so grand,
Constructs a castle made of sand.

The giggles echo, bumblebees hum,
While hedgehogs waltz and beat the drum.
A pot of honey, sticky and bright,
Becomes a feast, oh what delight!

So wander deep, embrace the lore,
Where whimsy reigns forever more.
In the heart of green, it’s plain to see,
Nature’s laughter sets us free!

Pockets of Reflection

In puddles deep, the world's inverted,
Where frogs hold court, oh so diverted.
A dragonfly sings high and low,
While frogs respond with a ribbit show!

The reflections swirl, a dance of trees,
Where gossip flows upon the breeze.
A beetle preens with a stylish flair,
Admiring itself with utmost care.

In quiet nooks, the shadows sprawl,
Critters gather, having a ball.
A snail slides in, with a wink to share,
While all the while, there's laughter in the air!

So dip your toes in whimsical streams,
Unlock your heart to endless dreams.
In nature's mirror, bright and clear,
Embrace the laughter, feel the cheer!

Sprigs of Solitude

In a forest of giggles, I take a walk,
My shadow fumbles, unable to talk.
Branches do ballet, leaves start to sway,
Whispering secrets of their crazy play.

Squirrels in headphones dance on a limb,
Raccoons join in, but their style's quite grim.
The sunlight chuckles, the breeze plays a tune,
While a nut drops down, and I summon a swoon.

The trunks gossip loudly, sharing old lore,
About the great hoot of the wise old owl's snore.
Tickling the bark, a subtle breeze winks,
While the grass below silently thinks.

Oh, solitude's dance is a wild, fun scene,
In this quirky grove, confusion is keen.
Left alone with laughter, who could complain?
Nature's humorous roots drive me half insane!

The Symphony of Splintered Stems

Hark! The woodlands beckon, a concert awaits,
With branches as conductors, they orchestrate dates.
Leaves flap a rhythm; the ground keeps the beat,
While twigs form a chorus—listen, it's neat!

The rustling crescendo of beetles in string,
Fluttering bugs join with a musical zing.
Moss hums a low tune beneath mighty oaks,
As laughter erupts from the forest, it chokes.

A cacophony clamors—a snapping twig band,
Dancing around in a tall-timbered land.
Old roots play the bass, and the flowers hum high,
While the stumps tap their feet to the clouds in the sky.

Such joy in this mess of splinter and song,
Who knew that the forest could jam all night long?
Lost in the melody of twigs playing great,
I'll dance in the rhythm and savor this fate!

Petals of Forgotten Stories

Whispers of petals float through the air,
Carrying tales of mishaps and flair.
An ant learned to tango, a bee told a joke,
All while the daisies just giggled and croaked.

Once a lost leaf thought it could fly,
But wind took a turn, and it waved goodbye.
A blossom once blushed, now forgot by the sun,
Hanging with twigs, having too much fun.

The lawn chairs remember when weeds had a ball,
While dandelion dreams took over it all.
But fading to memory can often be sweet,
As blooms laugh about how "life's still a treat!"

Gather round for a chat; nature's got style,
With stories of gnarly mishaps that reconcile.
In this patchwork of blooms, we dance and we sing,
As petals keep whispering of colorful things!

In the Shadow of Saplings

Under the shade of sprightly young trees,
I sip on my lemonade, feeling the breeze.
Their awkward attempts at growing upright,
Makes me laugh out loud—they're a humorous sight!

A sapling named Gary thinks he's quite grand,
But wobbles and sways in the soft-handed land.
His leaves seem to dance, but let's not be fooled,
For wind's just a prankster; oh how he's ruled!

While smaller ones gossip, holding their leaves tight,
Who knew a twig could spark such a delight?
On rocks, beetles giggle at the cats and their plight,
As shadows stretch long, making day turn to night.

So here in the garden of wobbly fun,
Each sapling's a jester, each leaf weighs a ton.
Laughter bends branches, and all nature sings,
In the twinkling twilight, it invents silly things!

Forgotten Stories of the Forest Floor

Beneath the leaves, they whisper loud,
Tiny tales of a nature crowd.
Squirrels plot with acorn plans,
While mushrooms dance in leafy bands.

A beetle burps, a worm does waltz,
In this realm, each frolic faults.
Old logs laugh, their gnarled grins,
Holding secrets of tiny sins.

A hedgehog snorts, a snail's slow crawl,
Each loves to boast, but none are tall.
In this chaos, joy unfolds,
As mystery dizzies, as fun it holds.

So take a look, be sure to tread,
Where magic swirls, and nonsense led.
A forest floor of fun and cheers,
Its vivid laughter spans the years.

Crickets and Cracks

Crickets chirp a melody,
While branches sway, so tenderly.
Each crack of wood, a laugh so sweet,
Nature's jokes, a grand repeat.

A rabbit hops, a dance nearby,
With wiggly ears, it's quite spry.
But watch your step on roots so sly,
Or meet your fate as you fly high!

Mice scamper as the shadows grow,
With secret paths where few may go.
Their tiny giggles fill the air,
In eerie light, without a care.

So in the night, when crickets rhyme,
Find laughter woven through their chime.
It's funny how each crack and squeak,
Makes happiness seem less unique.

Entwined Through Time

Vines twist tales of days gone by,
They kink and curl with no goodbye.
A squirrel’s journey, a fox's spree,
Their history shared with glee.

Branches hug in playful tease,
While ferns flail in a gentle breeze.
A ladybug spins giddy twirls,
In a dance that gives us swirls.

Each bark a story, knots and bends,
With giggles from long-lost friends.
Oh don’t forget that snail with charm,
Its pace so slow, it brings no harm.

So if you wander, take your time,
Listen close, perhaps a rhyme.
Nature's jests, both old and new,
Entwined in laughter just for you.

Shadows of the Woodland

In shadows deep, the mischief brews,
A leaf falls down, a prank it views.
A fox tiptoes, with sneaky glee,
Chasing shadows that tease the tree.

Ghostly owls with wise old eyes,
Chat with critters of lowly size.
Each rustle and giggle, a tale to weave,
In twilight's cloak, they'll never leave.

A shadow hops, a flicker bright,
Disguised as dance, in dim moonlight.
The laughter echoes through the wood,
In splashes of fun, where mischief stood.

So roam the paths where shadows play,
Join the laughter that's here to stay.
In woodland stories that softly thrive,
It's where enchantment comes alive.

Divine Smallness

In gardens where the critters prance,
A pebble holds a grand romance.
A blade of grass, a windy dance,
While ants conduct a fine expanse.

Their world so vast, yet oh so small,
They laugh and play, they have a ball.
With acorns bright, they build a hall,
In nutty dreams, they stand so tall.

Who knew a thimble could be grand?
For mice, it's a luxurious land.
And when the moon is on the sand,
They sip their tea, so finely planned.

In this small realm, they are the kings,
On tiny thrones, they rule small things.
With little crowns and shimmered rings,
They jest and twirl; laughter springs.

The Intricacies of Leafy Lives

A leaf that flutters in the breeze,
Hides secrets shared with busy bees.
While snails debate who takes the tease,
The laughter in the trees will please.

The creeping vines weave tales so tall,
One leaf says, 'Hey, you're quite the sprawl!'
They giggle softly, start to brawl,
As shadows dance and daylight stalls.

A conga line of ants go by,
A curious beetle bellies high.
In nature's map, they flutter nigh,
While thorns and petals wave goodbye.

The drummers, crickets, hum a tune,
While petals twirl beneath the moon.
In silent whispers, oh so soon,
They spin their tales of leafy swoon.

The Heartbeat of Tiny Things

Listen close to nature's hum,
A tiny world, a gentle drum.
The buzzing bee, it’s never glum,
While ladybugs do just become!

The fireflies light up the night,
Tiny flickers, pure delight.
With winks and blinks, they claim their right,
In this small realm, all is bright.

The clams approach for a small chat,
'Have you heard the news, dear brat?'
They speak of tides, and where they sat,
In bubbles full of giggles—fat!

The heartbeat of these minuscule things,
A symphony like joy that rings.
With tiny voices, woodland sings,
A world of wonders, fun it brings!

Cradles of Life's Secrets

In mossy cushions, whispers hide,
A treasure trove where dreams collide.
Where tiny mice do not abide,
In cradles soft, they swell with pride.

The wiggly worms have quite the tales,
About the snails' long, slippery trails.
They gossip 'neath the shady pales,
As dandelions blow sweet gales.

The wise old snail, a crusty sage,
Gives life advice with slowest gauge.
While beetles vouch for every page,
They laugh about the nursery stage.

With every seed, a dance begins,
A cycle twirls, life never thins.
In cradle soft, the laughter spins,
In tiny worlds, joy always wins.

The Language of Twirling Vines

In a garden where whispers play,
Vines twirl in a most peculiar way.
They gossip and giggle as they entwine,
Flirting with sunlight, feeling divine.

Bugs join in with a joyful hum,
Discussing their plans for the upcoming fun.
Leaves join the chatter with rustling cheer,
It's a botanical party, loud and clear!

Petals pop out with a wink and a nudge,
Waving at wind, they refuse to budge.
Root systems chuckle beneath the ground,
In this green ballroom, hilarity's found.

And while the world fumbles through the day,
The vines keep themselves in a playful ballet.
Nature’s amusement is no small feat,
Dancing to rhythms that can’t be beat!

Hidden Paths in Verdant Realms

In a forest where shadows flicker and play,
Paths twist and turn like a child at play.
With branches all laughing, what a sight,
Leading lost wanderers into delight.

Squirrels race wildly, hoarding their stash,
While rabbits pause for a sudden dash.
The thickets giggle as they conspire,
To lead all the wanderers into the mire.

With each curious nook, there's a prank to behold,
Moss-wrapped stones that sparkle like gold.
The trails seem to whisper, "Will you stay?"
As they wiggle mischievously, leading the way.

But once you embrace nature's cheeky game,
You'll find secret joys that call out your name.
Amidst the greenery, adventure is real,
In hidden paths, you learn how to feel!

The Dance of Petite Limbs

The dance floor made of twigs and leaves,
Invites the smallest to show their all.
Ants do the cha-cha, bugs lead the jive,
While the tiny trees sing, all come alive.

A ladybug spins in her polka-dot suit,
With a pirouette, she steals the salute.
Grasshoppers leap like they own the space,
Each one a star in this leafy embrace.

Mice tap their feet to the music of night,
With shadows that dance, oh what a sight!
Petite limbs waggle, waving with glee,
In this grand gala of nature, so free.

With laughter and chirps, the chorus sings on,
As dusk turns to twilight, no need to yawn.
Oh, the joy in this dance, where the tiny take flight,
In the moonlight they twirl, a delightful sight!

Soft Cradles of the Earth

The ground bugs giggle, soft pillows of green,
Where wildflowers fumble, a colorful scene.
Each petal a wink, each leaf a tease,
Cradling dreams in the gentlest breeze.

Worms throw a party; they roll and they squish,
Who knew earth could have such a funky wish?
With tiny confetti, they wiggle and squirm,
A muddy affair filled with joyful charm.

Fungi in hats tap dance on logs,
Whispering secrets to curious frogs.
With each soft cradle, laughter does swell,
As the earth tickles gently, casting its spell.

In cozy nooks where the wild things hide,
Magic's at play in the mud and the tide.
So come join the fun, get lost in the mirth,
In these soft cradles, the joys of the earth!

Skeletons of Seasons Past

In the yard the bones do dance,
Old branches trying to romance.
Leaves that fell, a scattered feast,
In secret whispers, they're released.

Rattling songs of autumn love,
From every twig that fate's approved.
A scary sight, the kids won't lie,
When ghosts of summer saunter by.

The winter chill, it gives a shiver,
While conifers stand tall, they quiver.
Yet somehow, it's a cheerful show,
As skeletons make quite the row.

So raise a toast, to what we've lost,
In every branch, remember the cost.
The laughter echoes, as they fall,
In nature's jest, we now enthrall.

The Language of Leafless Trees

What do the branches say at night?
"Let's throw a party, get it right!"
The trunks all chuckle, bark in glee,
In their own tongue, like gossiping tea.

The clouds drift past, mischief in tow,
Offering shade for the funny show.
With every rustle, a giggle shared,
In a world where no one is scared.

Twigs perform, a delicate play,
Where shadows mingle, come what may.
"Shall we sway, let the breezes tease?"
The trees unite as if to please.

So when you wander, stop and hear,
The silly stories that touch the ear.
For in their silence, humor we'll find,
Among leaves lost, what's left behind.

Twisted Chronicles of the Forest

Oh, the tales that branches tell,
Of summer storms and where they fell.
Bending low, they twist and weave,
A comedy of bark, you won't believe.

There's a squirrel who claims to be the king,
While acorns gather, plotting their fling.
Through tangled roots and tangled dreams,
Nature scribbles her funny memes.

A rabbit hops, a fox does prance,
Collecting twigs as they join the dance.
The moonlight giggles, plays a tune,
With shadows leaping beneath the moon.

In this forest, laughter reigns,
As twigs collide and sanity wanes.
So heed the whispers, don't let it pass,
In nature's opera, there's always sass.

The Poetry of Fragile Growth

In the cradle of dirt, they sprout with glee,
Soft little whispers, “Look at me!”
The sprouts wobble, their dance so light,
While bugs applaud, all feeling bright.

Their stems entwine, a silly affair,
With giggles shared, they don’t have a care.
They stretch and grow, absurdly bold,
In nature's book, their stories unfold.

Frogs croak verses, a chorus so pure,
With rhymes about growth, and dreams that endure.
In every droplet, they see the skies,
Where every flower has its own surprise.

So as you wander down the lane,
Remember the humor that grows with the rain.
For even the smallest, when all is told,
Knows how to giggle, even when bold.

The Lightness of Lichen

On branches, the green fuzz grows,
A party for bugs, I suppose.
They wiggle and jiggle around,
In a microscopic playground.

It tickles the bark like a joke,
An ancient life form, no spoke.
Whispers of laughter in bark,
Where moss and humor leave their mark.

They sway with the breeze, having fun,
Bouncing along as if on the run.
A dance of the odd and the sleek,
Nature’s commotion, a laugh by the creek.

Living the life of a party scene,
With no need for curtains to preen.
In their own world, no need to be wise,
Just a patch of cheer under blue skies.

Veins of the Verdant

In the forest, where sunshine beams,
The greenery bursts forth with dreams.
Leaves chuckle under a tickling breeze,
As squirrels conspire with playful ease.

Grass blades gossip and sway with cheer,
Whispering secrets that no one can hear.
Nature's own gossip, oh what a thrill,
Each wrinkle and vein has a story to spill.

Between colors that twinkle and dance,
Every leaf flaunts its prancing romance.
The vines all tangle in a playful race,
With snickers and giggles, they pick up the pace.

A canvas of laughter painted so bright,
The earth holds its jokes till the last bit of light.
In a tapestry woven of green and of glee,
The veins of the verdant set laughter free.

Labyrinth of Lost Limbs

In the woods, where branches play hide and seek,
Fallen limbs lie like chairs for the meek.
They giggle and chatter, the roots underground,
With stories of journeys, they swirl all around.

A maze of old twigs, where tales intertwine,
Each twist and turn feels like sipping fine wine.
A foot here, a hand there, all lost in the fray,
In branches of laughter, they tumble and sway.

The ghosts of old trees tell jokes to the sky,
As critters debate who will be the next spy.
They dangle and sway in their tangled embrace,
In a riddle of limbs, there's always a space.

So wander and ponder where pathways might lead,
In this playful maze where nature's a steed.
With each wobbly step on this quirky old trail,
Laughter erupts, and joy will prevail.

Echoing the Essence of Eden

In a garden where whimsy meets shade,
Echoes of laughter in every glade.
Flowers with faces, they wink and they nod,
Sharing secrets with each blushing clod.

The vines hang low, stretching out for a tease,
In their soft whispers, they tickle the trees.
Petals like giggles float down to the ground,
In this jester's abode, joy's always found.

Bees buzzing tunes while they swirl with delight,
As butterflies play tag, oh what a sight!
In a world where the trivial turns into gold,
The essence of laughter, forever retold.

With sunbeam confetti that brightens the day,
Eden's own humor comes out to play.
Gather your chuckles, collect them with care,
In this joyous realm, there's laughter to share.

Patterns of Ancestral Twigs

In the forest, odd shapes loom,
Branches twist like a child's cartoon.
Grandpa's nose, it surely shows,
A family tree where laughter grows.

Long-lost aunts, with hats askew,
Dance with squirrels, it's quite the view.
Uncles boast of their tree-climbing fame,
While cousins argue about the game.

Leaves whisper secrets, oh what a sight,
Dancing around in the dappled light.
Fables spun from bark and twig,
All rooted deep, where the stories dig.

So raise a toast, let's not be shy,
To our family's quirks, oh my, oh my!
Patterns so wild, they twist and spin,
In this crazy forest, let laughter begin.

Light Passes Through Wood

Sunbeams play peek-a-boo today,
With shadows that hop, skip, and sway.
Wooden wonders, where do you grow?
Tickling the light, putting on a show.

Branches stretch like they're on vacation,
While beams of sunlight hold a conversation.
Splinters are giggling, acting quite bold,
As laughter warms up the air, uncontrolled.

Knots have their stories, twisted so neat,
Telling all tales, oh how they compete!
Whispers through bark, a comedy spree,
Each joke crafted perfectly, like an old tree.

So let us bask in this wooden dome,
Where silly critters call their home.
As light pours in, the fun unfurls,
In this lively wood, laughter twirls.

The Grains of Time

In the depths of the woods, time takes a trip,
With grains that tell tales of a squirrel's flip.
Beneath the bark, giggles are stored,
Each ring a story, hold your applause!

Years pile up like a game of stacks,
Where every wobble, a heartwarming laugh backs.
A knot in the wood, all tangled and gruff,
"Who needs a groom when you're this tough?"

So count those rings, one, two, three, four,
To find the joker hiding beneath the door.
Tick-tocking trees, what ruckus you bring,
As we dance through the ages, let merriment sing!

Relax with the grains, they're more than mere wood,
They've seen love, they've seen joy, they've seen all that they could.
Through laughter and grooves, time's not so grim,
In the grains of our lives, let joy never dim!

Creatures of the Subtle

In the shadows dwell creatures so sly,
Whiskers twitching, oh my! Oh my!
With eyes like buttons and fur like the night,
They plot all their pranks in the pale moonlight.

A beetle wears glasses, wise as can be,
Telling jokes to a snail, slow as can see.
While chipmunks conduct their wild little band,
Singing tunes that no one can understand.

Mystery lurks under each leafy shroud,
Giggles echo where the woods feel proud.
Bugs and their tricks make life quite a game,
With every rustle, they're calling your name.

So join in the fun before the moon fades,
With creatures that laugh in the woodland glades.
For in these soft whispers and giggles so cute,
Lies a world of tomfoolery, life's sweetest loot.

Little Echoes of Eternity

In a forest where whispers play,
Little critters dance all day.
Squirrels juggling acorns, oh so spry,
While bees wear tiny hats and fly.

Even the mushrooms seem to tease,
Tickling the toes of the wandering breeze.
A raccoon in shades with a cheeky grin,
As leaves start to giggle, they join in the din.

The sunbeams chuckle, bright and bold,
While shadows scheme for treasures untold.
Each branch has a story, some silly, some wise,
In a world where the mundane often flies.

So listen closely to the banter and jokes,
For even the pine trees have their strokes.
In this playful realm where laughter rings,
Eternity echoes with the joy it brings.

Fragile Sentinels

Up in the treetops, flat on the ground,
Little sentinels stand all around.
With capes made of leaves and crowns of delight,
They joke with the wind through day and night.

A twigged soldier marches in line,
Winks at a beetle sipping on brine.
With twirling mustaches, the dandelions grin,
As butterflies come in for a spin.

They guard tiny treasures, like pebbles and crumbs,
And chuckle at ants while they carry their sums.
In their world of minuscule charm and grace,
Life is a game, a whimsical race.

So when you wander through twiggy domains,
Remember the laughter that softly remains.
For these fragile sentinels, proud and spry,
Turn moments of life into jokes on the fly.

Journeys of the Small

Once upon a forest path, so wide,
A crew of small creatures set off to glide.
With a map made of leaves and snacks in tow,
Adventure awaited with wonders to show.

A snail was the captain, so wise and grand,
While the ants formed a band, quite out of hand.
They sang silly songs and danced through the glade,
While picking up stories of the choices they made.

They crossed over puddles with comedic flair,
As crickets crooned tunes from the tall grass lair.
Each leap and each tumble brought giggles anew,
In a journey where everything felt brightly askew.

So tread softly, dear travelers, and join in the cheer,
For the journeys of small ones are magic, I fear.
Each shuffle, each giggle, each quirky surprise,
Shows us that joy is in the small and the wise.

Understory Chronicles

In the depths of the thicket, where shadows flit,
Lives a world of giggles and playful wit.
From worms in tuxedos to beetles on stage,
They scribble their stories on nature's own page.

A hedgehog in boots tries to tango and spin,
While twigs crack jokes about their own kin.
With whispers of petals and rustles of grass,
They hold a grand ball for the critters that pass.

Fireflies flash like disco lights in the dark,
As everyone gathers at this festooned park.
With laughter erupting from every small soul,
In this understory realm, they embody the whole.

So pause as you wander beneath boughs so thick,
And hear the shenanigans, the laughter, the trick.
For in this hidden chronicle, bright and divine,
The joy of the tiny is truly the sign.

The Universe Within Twigs

In the forest, secrets lie,
A universe beneath the sky.
Twigs like rockets, flying high,
Count the stars, let worries fly.

The ants are astronauts, how they march,
On their tiny, twirling arch.
Every twig's a spaceship, if you see,
Taking laughter far and free.

Branches whisper jokes to leaves,
While playful winds do tricks like thieves.
Nature’s humor fills the air,
Twigs giggle in a cosmic affair.

So grab a twig, it’s quite bizarre,
Pretend you’re flying, it’s not far!
With a snicker and a play,
Twigs will take you far away.

Dreams Resting on the Ground

Look down low, what do you see?
Dreams are sleeping, wild and free.
Pebbles grin, they're quite a site,
While twigs tell tales of day and night.

Rolled-up dreams lie underfoot,
Like little laughs, all spruced up.
Dance of slumber, a giggling land,
Awake and joyfully, take a stand.

Stick figures dance in silent cheer,
While mossy cushions draw you near.
Whimsical thoughts in earthy beds,
Twigs weave dreams for happy heads.

Nature's playground holds delight,
In every twig, a spark of light.
So step on dreams, without a sound,
And wake them up from underground.

Messages Carried by Nature

Twigs are letters, short and sweet,
Carrying whispers, oh so neat.
Messages from the wise old oak,
In every crack, a little joke.

Squirrels read them, chuckling loud,
Sharing tales with the merry crowd.
The wind's a postman, swift and sly,
Delivering giggles that flutter by.

Rustling leaves join in the fun,
Sending messages, just begun.
A twig's a shout, a leaf's a grin,
Nature's letters, let the fun begin!

So tune your ears to nature's call,
Those tiny twigs know joy for all.
Read and laugh, what a delight,
Messages of giggles, day and night.

The Balance of Small Things

In a world so big, we often miss,
The power in small things, pure bliss.
A dash of joy, a sprinkle of wit,
With tiny twigs, you can't quit!

Balance is found in a little dance,
A bounce on twigs gives joy a chance.
Nature's humor, in every sway,
Tiny adventures lead the way.

A twig for balance, a leaf to play,
Every small giggle brightens the day.
So skip along, don't miss a chance,
To find delight in nature's dance.

With each small thing, life's not so grand,
But full of laughter, hand in hand.
So gather twigs, let spirits rise,
In the balance found, the funny lies.

www.ingramcontent.com/pod-product-compliance
Lightning Source LLC
Chambersburg PA
CBHW072146200426
43209CB00051B/751
* 9 7 8 1 8 0 5 6 7 2 8 1 4 *